DIGGING UP THE PAST

BOG BODIES

BY TRUDY BECKER

WWW.APEXEDITIONS.COM

Apex is distributed by North Star Editions:
sales@northstareditions.com | 888-417-0195

Produced for Apex by Red Line Editorial.

Photographs ©: Heribert Proepper/AP Images, cover; Sven Rosborn/Wikimedia Commons, 1, 22–23; Shutterstock Images, 4–5, 6–7, 9, 10–11, 12, 14–15, 21; Ian Dagnall/Alamy, 8; Julien Behal/PA Images/Alamy, 13; Dpa Picture Alliance Archive/Alamy, 16–17; C. M. Dixon/Print Collector/Hulton Archive/Getty Images, 19; Gene J. Puskar/AP Images, 20, 29; iStockphoto, 24; Christian Kober/robertharding/Alamy, 25; WHPics/Alamy, 26; McLeod/Wikimedia Commons, 27

Library of Congress Control Number: 2024952837

ISBN
979-8-89250-530-7 (hardcover)
979-8-89250-566-6 (paperback)
979-8-89250-636-6 (ebook pdf)
979-8-89250-602-1 (hosted ebook)

Printed in the United States of America
Mankato, MN
082025

NOTE TO PARENTS AND EDUCATORS

Apex books are designed to build literacy skills in striving readers. Exciting, high-interest content attracts and holds readers' attention. The text is carefully leveled to allow students to achieve success quickly. Additional features, such as bolded glossary words for difficult terms, help build comprehension.

TABLE OF CONTENTS

CHAPTER 1

A BODY BELOW

In May 1950, a family walks through a **bog** near Silkeborg, Denmark. They have a job to do. They are collecting **peat**.

People cut peat out of bogs. Once the peat dries, people can burn it for heat and cooking.

The family's shovels cut deep into the spongy ground. Suddenly, they hit something. A human body is stuck in the bog. It looks fresh. They tell the police.

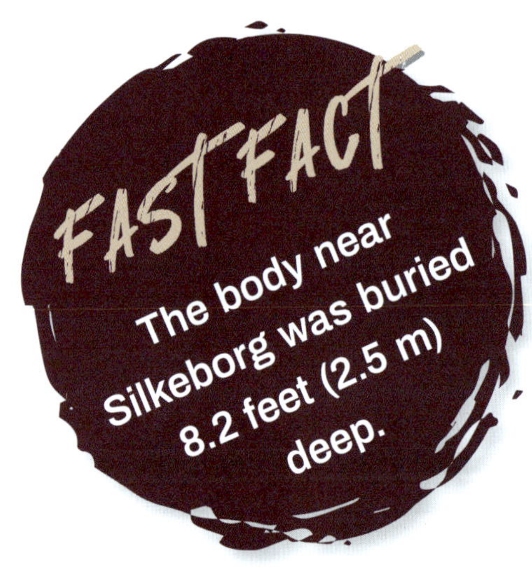

Because it was buried in a bog, the body's skin had turned a dark color. But it did not rot.

The body had a rope around his neck. Scientists think he was hanged.

The police rush to the scene. Museum workers come, too. They take a closer look. This is no recent crime. The man died more than 2,000 years ago.

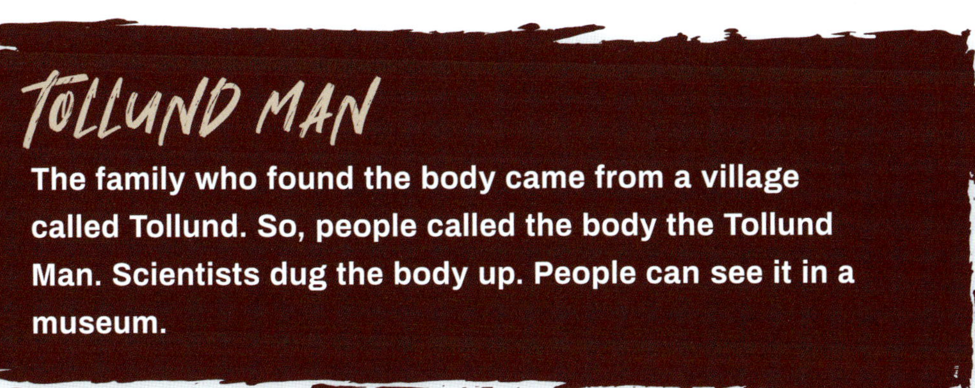

TOLLUND MAN

The family who found the body came from a village called Tollund. So, people called the body the Tollund Man. Scientists dug the body up. People can see it in a museum.

The Tollund Man is in the Museum Silkeborg in Denmark.

CHAPTER 2

WHAT ARE BOG BODIES?

Bog bodies are old bodies preserved in wetlands. The bodies were buried in the swampy ground. Peat kept them from breaking down.

In 1938, people found a woman's body in Denmark. The bog preserved her braided hair.

Many bogs are cold. They have little oxygen. They have lots of **acid** and sphagnum moss, too. These things stop **bacteria** from growing. Bacteria make dead things rot.

When sphagnum moss dies, it becomes peat. It also adds more acid to bogs.

Bogs preserve items such as metal weapons very well, even over many years.

FOUND IN THE BOG

Bogs can preserve old items, too. Scientists have found wood, clothes, and even food. Ancient people may have used bogs to keep food cold.

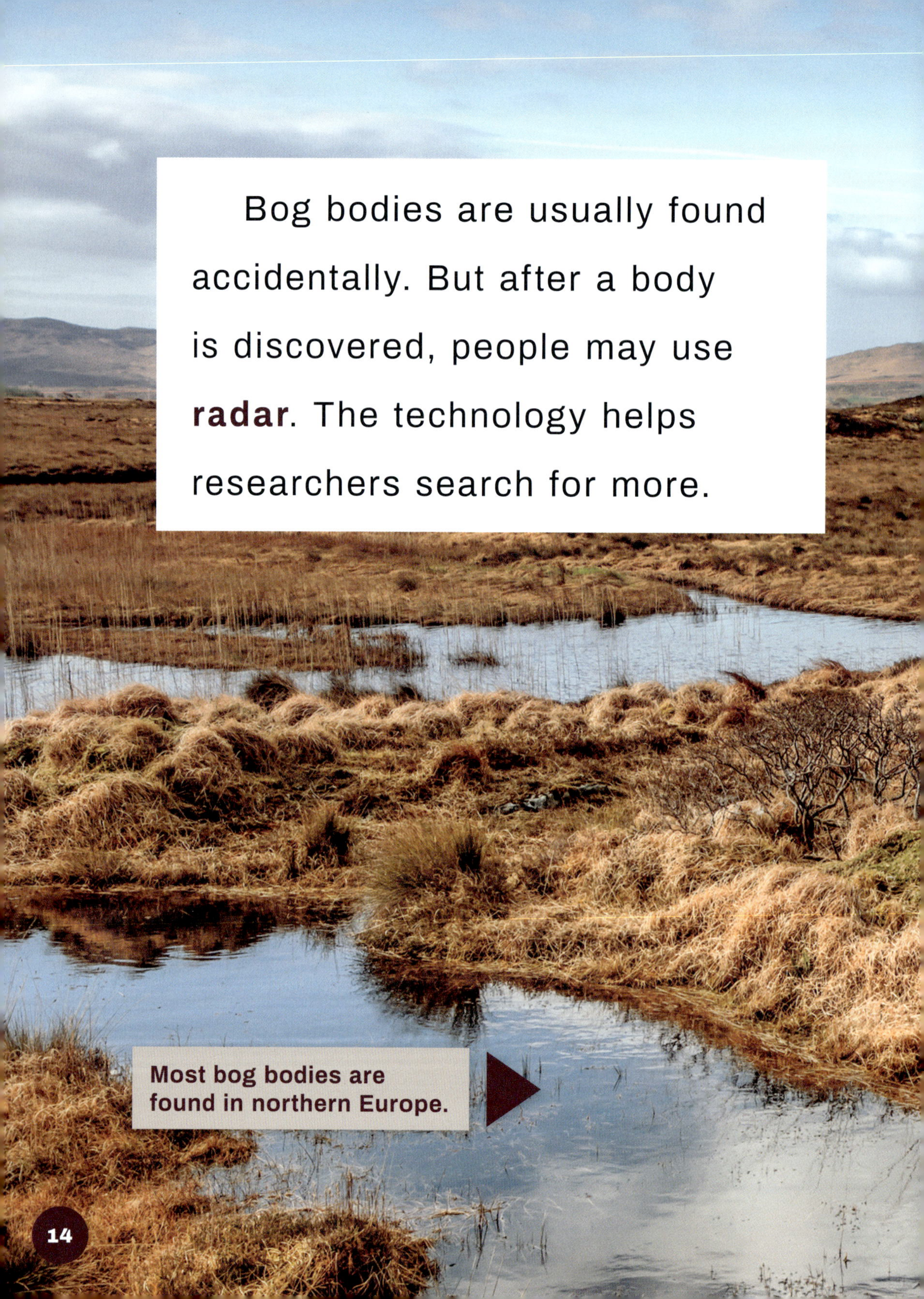

Bog bodies are usually found accidentally. But after a body is discovered, people may use **radar**. The technology helps researchers search for more.

Most bog bodies are found in northern Europe.

FAST FACT

Since the 1600s, people have discovered hundreds of bog bodies.

CHAPTER 3

SECRETS IN THE BOG

Scientists gather many details from bog bodies. For example, they can find out a body's age and gender. They study and scan the bones.

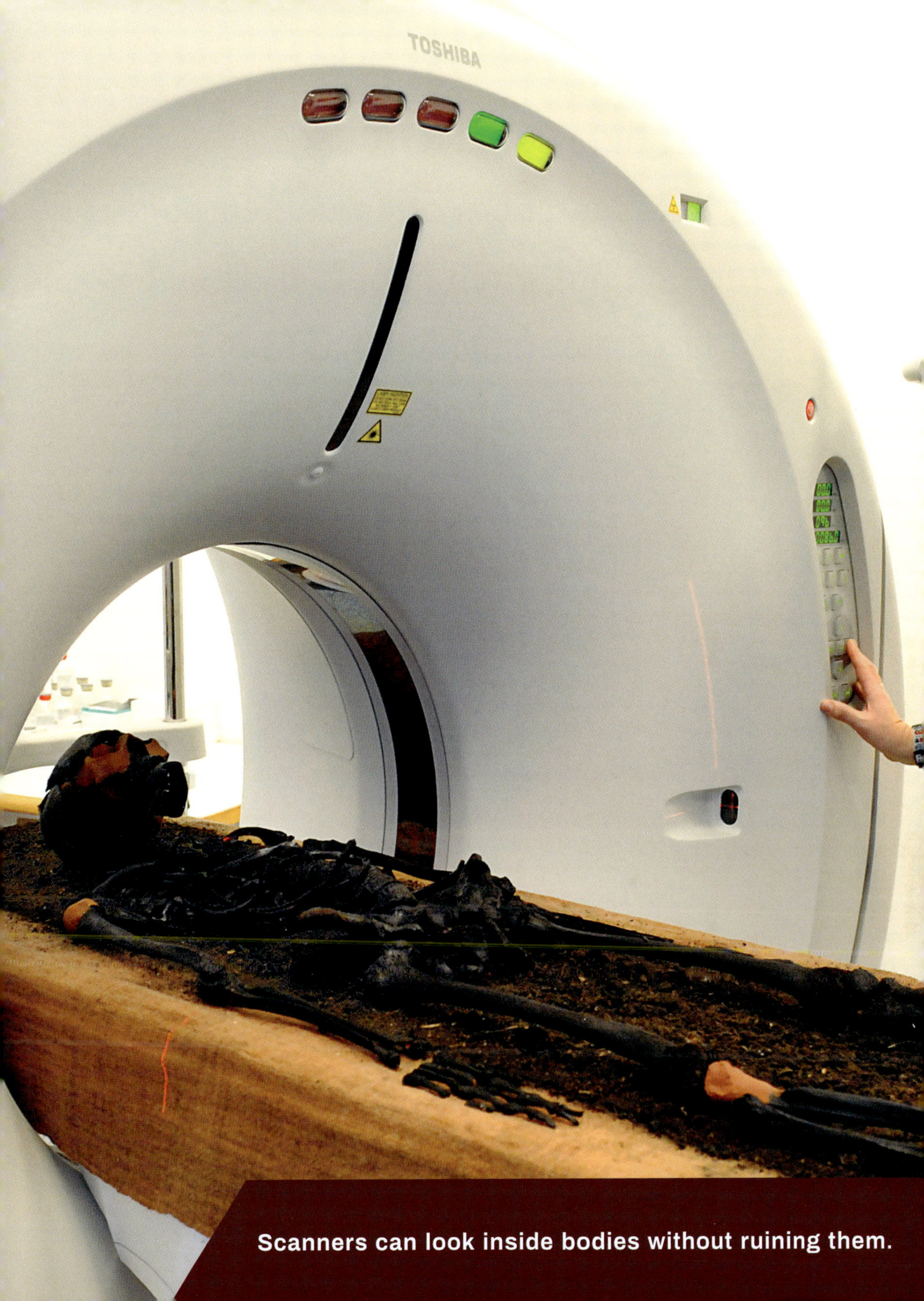

Scanners can look inside bodies without ruining them.

Researchers often use carbon to find out when people died. They take this chemical from hair, bones, or other body parts. As of 2024, the Koelbjerg Man was the oldest bog body found. His bones date to 8000 BCE.

LINDOW MAN

In the 1980s, people found the Lindow Man in Cheshire, England. He died around 2,100 years ago. He was about 25 years old.

The Lindow Man had a broken neck and many cuts.

The Yde Girl was found in the Netherlands. She was around 16 years old when she died.

Researchers learn how people died, too. Many bog bodies have wounds. They may have been **sacrificed**. The Yde Girl is one example. She was strangled and stabbed in the neck.

FAST FACT

In some **cultures**, bogs were **sacred** places.

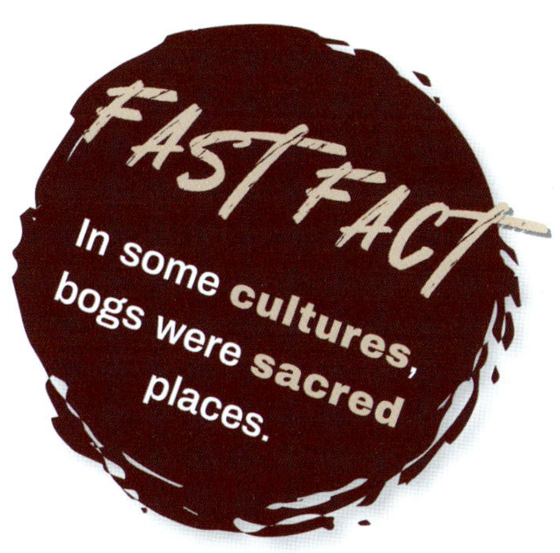

Some ancient people saw bogs as links to the world of gods and goddesses.

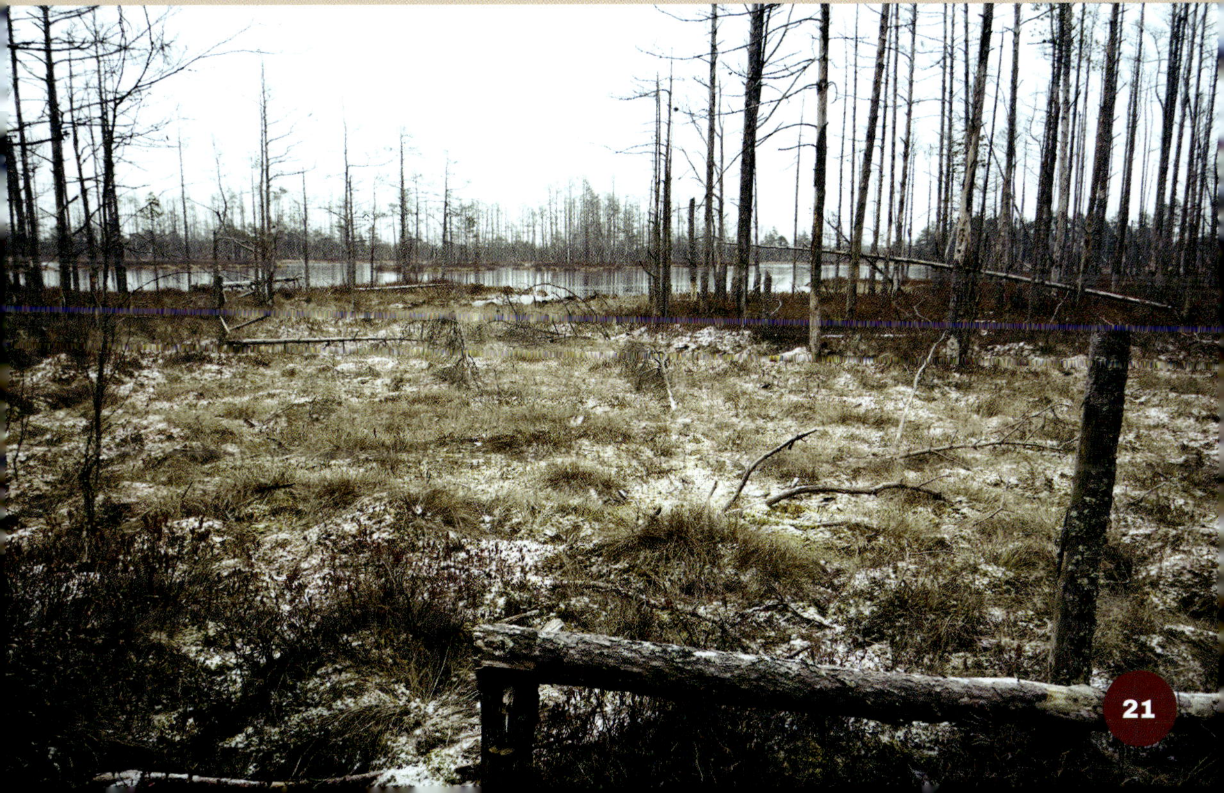

CHAPTER 4

TESTS AND TRACES

Bog bodies help people understand ancient cultures. For example, some bodies are found wearing clothes. Others have traces of fabric. Both show what ancient people wore.

The Huldremose Woman was found in Denmark. She wore a skirt, scarf, and two capes.

The stomachs of some bodies contain food. Scientists can see what type. That helps them learn the foods ancient people ate.

Researchers found that the Tollund Man ate porridge and fish before he died.

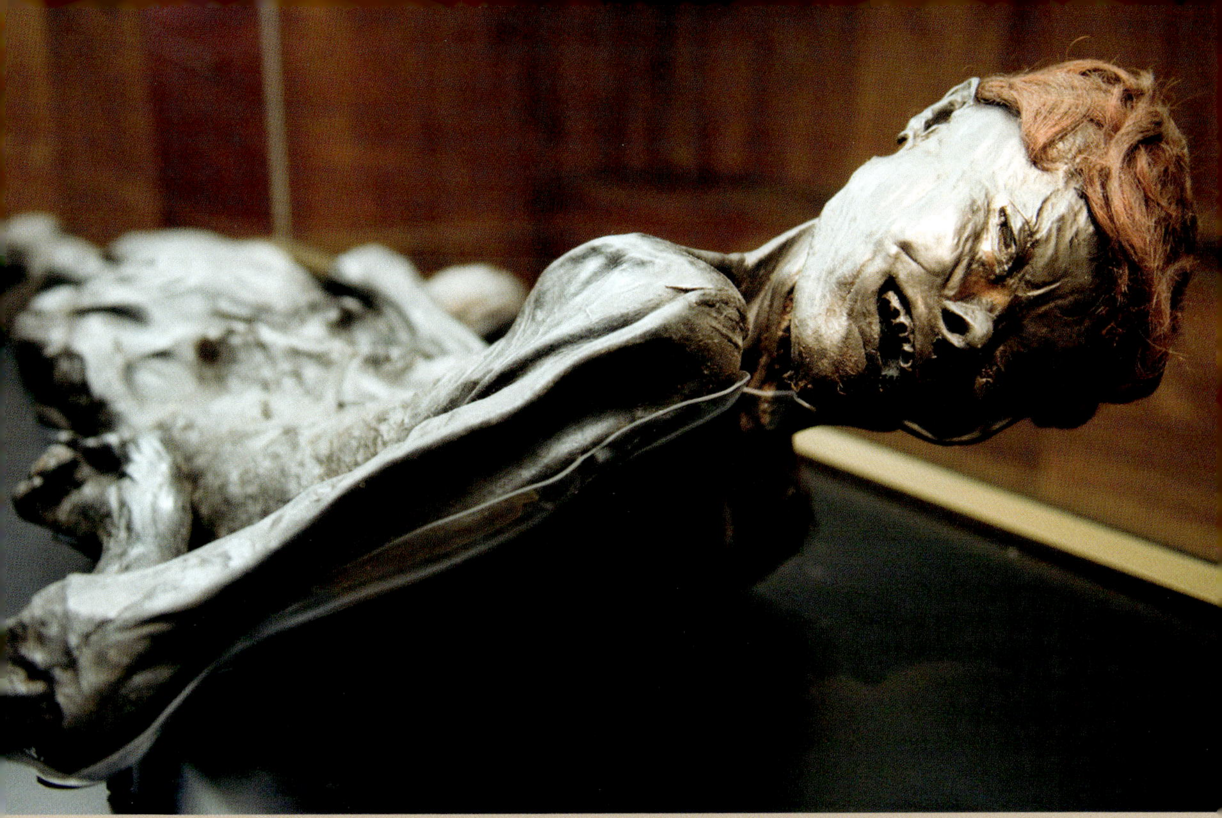

In the 1950s, scientists studied the Grauballe Man's teeth. They found that he ate mostly grains.

FAST FACT

Over time, the hair on bog bodies turns red.

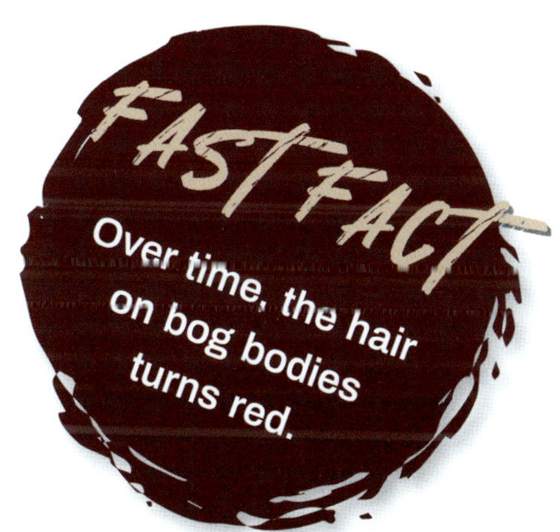

Some models are made by computers. Others are built from wax or clay.

Researchers study **DNA** from the bodies, too. They take it from hair, bones, skin, or teeth. They get details about how the person looked. Researchers can make models of the people.

TRAVELING FAR

The Haraldskaer Woman was found in Denmark. A scientist tested a chemical in her hair. It showed that she had made a long trip before dying.

The Haraldskaer Woman's body is about 2,200 years old.

COMPREHENSION QUESTIONS

Write your answers on a separate piece of paper.

1. Write a few sentences describing one thing that people can learn by studying bog bodies.

2. Would you want to see a bog body in a museum? Why or why not?

3. Where was the Lindow Man found?

- **A.** Denmark
- **B.** England
- **C.** the Netherlands

4. Which place might preserve bodies the best?

- **A.** a bog with little moss
- **B.** a bog with lots of bacteria
- **C.** a bog with little heat

5. What does **recent** mean in this book?

*This is no **recent** crime. The man died more than 2,000 years ago.*

A. buried
B. new
C. tall

6. What does **fabric** mean in this book?

*For example, some bodies are found wearing clothes. Others have traces of **fabric**. Both show what ancient people wore.*

A. light
B. cloth
C. sound

Answer key on page 32.

GLOSSARY

acid

A strong chemical that often causes reactions.

bacteria

Tiny living things.

bog

An area of wet, spongy ground with lots of acid.

cultures

Groups of people and the ways they live, including their beliefs and laws.

DNA

A chemical in the body that is unique to each person.

peat

Material in bogs formed by dying plants.

radar

A system that sends out radio waves to locate objects.

sacred

Having close ties to a god, goddess, or religion.

sacrificed

Offered to gods or goddesses to win their favor.

BOOKS

Berne, Emma Carlson. *Mummies Around the World*. Lerner Publications, 2024.

Gaertner, Meg. *Stonehenge*. Apex Editions, 2022.

Murray, Julie. *Ötzi the Iceman*. Abdo Publishing, 2022.

ONLINE RESOURCES

Visit **www.apexeditions.com** to find links and resources related to this title.

ABOUT THE AUTHOR

Trudy Becker lives in Minneapolis, Minnesota. She likes books and exploring new places. She has never found a bog body.

INDEX

ANSWER KEY:
1. Answers will vary; 2. Answers will vary; 3. B; 4. C; 5. B; 6. B